COUNT IT ALL JOY

By Katrina B. Fonville

Printed in the United States of America.
Library of Congress

ISBN: 978-0-9985185-4-1

Fonville Publishing, P. O. Box 35893. Richmond, VA 23235

Note from the Author

This book, Count It All Joy, was birthed while going through some difficult times. Unfortunately, I did not have the foresight to journal or document everything that happened, so please have patience with me. My daughter kept telling me to write things down, but I believe the Holy Spirit will guide me as I go forth in writing this book.

The purpose of this book is to help you as life takes you through various trials and hard times. Hopefully, after reading this book you will go through your situations with a different attitude.

I want to thank my daughter, Lareesa Fonville, for gently nudging me to do this. Also, many thanks to Chief Apostle Olive C. Brown, the Presiding Prelate of International Christian Ministries, who inspires everyone to move forward in what God has for them. She has a way of bringing out the best in people. I've watched her over the years become a launching board for so many to reach their potential. I want to thank my Pastor, Bishop and Prophet Joel Vincent Brown of New Jerusalem International Christian Ministries who inspires me by his many messages, declarations, and impartations. I also want to thank my sons, Donnell and Earl, along with their families for all their love and support.

Table of Contents

Chapter 1
What Joy?

In life, we go through various circumstances. Highs and lows. Some will not only confuse you, but will blow your mind, and frustrate you. Some things will make absolutely no sense and leave you wondering why. It's during those challenging times, the Holy Spirit will say to me, "Count it all Joy." What I was going through didn't look like joy or feel like joy, but I went on with my life praying, trusting, and believing. But, all of a sudden, another situation! The Holy Spirit would say it again, "Count it all Joy." This would continuously happen off and on and I didn't understand why. You know how a building shakes during an earthquake? The shaking disrupts things a bit, but if the building is built with a strong enough foundation, it's likely to withstand the shaking. You may have to put your pictures back up on the walls or straighten up a little. But, the building didn't come crashing down. At times, it felt like my life was going through an earthquake. I didn't know how I was going to withstand the shaking or the broken pieces. But, I'm here to tell you God is a master at fixing things and, as God was stretching me, I learned how to count it all joy.

Quite a few years ago, I could not walk. I'm not sure what happened, but I found myself constantly hopping on one leg to get me from place to place. It was painful and frustrating. I remember sitting on the edge of my bed, trying to motivate myself to make the journey to the bathroom. It was only about 10 feet away, but it seemed so much further. I was tired of this condition. I was tired of this pain. I was so tired of not being able to use that leg, that I cried out to God with a loud voice, "Help Lord!!" I heard Him say, in a still soft voice, "That's all I wanted to hear." Immediately after that, I got up and walked normal without any pain!! Glory to God!!

That was a miracle!! I still believe in miracles. God was with me and He said He would never leave me nor forsake me. God is interested in our inner man and building us up inside. This built my faith and I will take this faith on to the next encounter. But, in that situation, that wasn't count it all joy. Maybe count it all pain or count it all inconvenience. But, not joy. I couldn't see the joy then. What I can say now, as I look back on my relationship with God, it was a learning experience for me. It was joy at the end when I cried out and He answered me, but up to that point it was not. God will work with you until you catch on. He takes us from faith to faith. He said when we call on Him, He would answer us. He will be with us in trouble and deliver us.

As I said, the Holy Spirit will say to me in many situations, "Count it all Joy." All situations were not that challenging. Some were more frustrating than anything else, but that's part of the ALL. We'll get more into that later, but for now, let's talk a little about the Holy Spirit.

For those who are not familiar with who the Holy Spirit is, I'm going to use some references from the Bible so you can look them up at leisure. Some call Him the Holy Ghost, others say Holy Spirit. Both are correct, as it is the Spirit of the Lord.

Your spirit becomes new when you invite Jesus in your heart. He gives you his righteousness and takes away your sins. That's salvation. Old things are passed away and all things are become new. (II Corinthians 5:17) Without the shedding of blood there is no remission of sin. Jesus paid the price on Calvary's cross so we may have eternal life with Him. If you have received Him, you have been born again and you are a new creature! You were born in sin thanks to the disobedience of Adam and Eve in the garden of Eden when they ate from the tree of knowledge and evil when they were told not to. (Genesis 2:17)

In the book of Acts, when the day of Pentecost had come Jesus disciples were gathered in the upper room, all on one accord waiting for the promise. They were told not to leave Jerusalem after the resurrection and to wait until they were endowed with power from on high. While they waited, there fell on them like fire cloven tongues and they were all filled with the Holy Spirit. Jesus, the savior of the world, now risen from the dead, and ascended into heaven and sat on the right hand of God, the Father, sent us His gift of His Spirit.

The Holy Spirit is our gift from God to help us to live a holy life and lead and guide us in this world. He reveals things to us and teaches us the things of God. He directs us and is our comforter and companion. Whatever He hears the Father says, that is what He says to us. (John 16:13)

Sometimes, when I am not even thinking about God at the time, just going about my way, the Holy Spirit interjects a comment on whatever I'm thinking about. He is such a gentleman. He will step back until you are ready for him. As you invite Him into every area of your life He will come there. But, if you quench the Spirit, He will step back. Some people may only want Him at church or in one part of their lives. But, I need Him all the time, in every area, and every second of every minute!!!

It's good to know He cares about whatever concerns us. But, sometimes, when He interjects, "Count it all Joy," I reply to Him, "Don't feel like joy, don't look like joy." My definition of joy must be wrong. This doesn't feel or look like joy at all. So, I went to the Bible and looked up the scripture in the book of James.

James 1:2 says, "My Brethren count it all joy when you fall into divers temptations." But, why should we count it ALL joy? Now doesn't that seem to go against the grain?!

Ok, wait. What exactly is joy? Greek dictionary definition:

cheerfulness, calm delight, gladness. Joy is a settled state of contentment, confidence, and hope. It is something or someone that provides a source of happiness.

I felt like I had none of the above. It was more like a state of hopelessness in that situation. I've learned that you can't go by feelings. That's why we need the Holy Spirit. Did you know within the fruit of the Spirit is Joy? The fruit of the Holy Spirit mentioned over in Galatians 5:22, is the result of the Holy Spirit's presence in the life of a Christian. It's already there.

In this next situation, it seemed like the roaring lion had just pounced, and it was very troubling to me. We must remember, in all our ways to acknowledge the Lord and

He will direct our paths. Had I done this, I believe I would've missed this encounter.

I wanted some work done to my house. Nothing major, but I thought I would try my neighbor's sons since I thought it was nice of one of them to ask me if he could do some work for me. These are grown men who visit their parents and do yardwork for them. We agreed on fixing and painting the front porch and cementing the driveway, where needed. I paid over half for the down payment before the work started. When it came to almost the end of the job, the boss brother wanted me to pay all the rest of the money before the job was complete. I disagreed because I wanted a finished product. This man made a huge scene on my front lawn with my son and me! He was extremely loud and very offensive! This was very embarrassing for me, as my other neighbors were also witnessing this. My son tried to calm him down. We had an agreement and this was business. But, he tried to make it seem like I was the bad guy and he was right. This was a hold your peace and let the Lord fight your battle situation. These brothers lived elsewhere, but their family lived across the street. I wanted to live in peace with them. I really wanted peace with the brothers as well. So, I counted it all joy. Their work was not good. I needed to have it redone, but I learned my lesson. We don't get it right the first time all the time. My neighbor and I still speak and are on good terms. I guess they know their son.

Although the situation was very disturbing to me, God was with me in it and through it. That is very important to remember. He will never leave you. God was with Daniel in the lion's den and with the Hebrew boys in the furnace. He was there. He was with Joseph when his brothers wanted to kill him and left him in the pit. In the end, God raised Joseph up to deliver these same brothers trying to do him in.

He used my son to be my advocate that day. In this situation, my peace was disturbed. The Bible tells us to be anxious for nothing. I had to get my peace back. God is not the author of confusion. So, I was being tried. God's Word Translation says, our suffering is light and temporary and is producing for us an eternal glory that is greater than anything we can imagine. God works things out for our good in this life and for the next whether it's within or without. We know it's all going to work out, somehow in his timing, so just start thanking God for the victory while you're going through. Better said than done, right? It takes coming to yourself sometimes to realize what's going on.

Some situations are not our plans and some are very uncomfortable. But the Bible says, many are the afflictions of the righteous, but God delivers us from them all.

Now these are light afflictions that I'm supposed to count all joy. The degrees of these light afflictions vary. Some will blow your mind, if you let them. Some can be brief encounters, pretty much caught off guard, some I can say I look back and laugh. These situations are building our dependence on God. They are building our communication with God. They are building our relationship with God. That's what He wants. He wants us to call on Him. He wants us to confide in Him. He wants us to know Him. We are learning to trust Him more. We are learning His ways. We are learning friendship and fellowship. We are learning we can depend on him.

Chapter 2
Why?

Let me explain a little about The Christian's life and God's kingdom. Christians are in God's kingdom and that kingdom is different from this world's system. It is a spiritual system. God is Spirit.

Let's start by looking at who we are. We are body, soul, and spirit. When we asked Jesus into our hearts we became new creatures. We have God's Spirit. We were born again. That part of us is new now.

As a Christian, even though we have a new spirit, we still have to renew our minds. Our thoughts get us in trouble sometimes. As a man thinks so is he. (Proverbs 23:7)

We have to learn the ways of God by reading and studying the Bible. As we learn and apply the Word of God (the Bible) to our lives we grow to be more like our Savior. Now we have Jesus who has ascended on high and is making intercession for us and we have the Holy Spirit in us if we have received this precious gift. We don't want to grieve him but please him in our thoughts and actions. We all error from time to time, but we should want to do better and ask the Holy Spirit to help us do better.

Before we were saved, our flesh led us. Whatever we felt like doing for the most part we did it. Now that we are saved, our born-again spirit should lead us. Sometimes through lust we are led astray by the flesh. The spirit man was not strong enough. The old saying is true. Seven days without prayer makes you weak. You've got to pray and read the Word every day and have communion with the Holy Spirit often so you'll get to know Him and be strong in God. This is necessary because the adversary, the devil, is out to catch you off guard. He is out to steal, kill, and destroy you. He is like a lion seeking whom he may devour and he will seek to hit you at your weakest point. I used to say I may be down, but I'm not out.

The government is on God's shoulder. (Isaiah 9:6) Yes, it is a government. There is order. In our government, we have rules and regulations and it's the same in God's kingdom. The first rule or commandment in God's kingdom is to love God with all your heart. The second rule or commandment is to love your neighbor as yourself (Mark 12:30-31). Many times, we may not want to love because something has happened, but God wants us to love our enemies and pray for those who despitefully use us. So sometimes we need help to do these things. We must will ourselves and let the feelings play catch up. Just do it God's way. It's the best way. He knows how to handle things. We think we do, but it is only because He gives us wisdom when we need it. Fearing God is the beginning of wisdom. (Proverbs 9:10)

Living on earth, we are in the world but not of the world. We live in the earth realm. Our flesh dominates this realm. Flesh says we're hungry so we eat, flesh says we're thirsty so we drink. Flesh says it's cloudy and rainy, so we're sad or depressed. People let the weather dominate their mood or even others. We listen to what others impose on us rather than listening to what God has to say about the situation. So, the flesh often wins.

But, what does the Word of God say? It says, we do not walk after the flesh, but after the Spirit. We are new creatures in Christ Jesus. We have been adopted into God's royal family. We must take God's yoke on us and learn from Him. (Matthew 11:29)

Since retiring, I've been working with my son in his

transportation business. Sometimes I get caught in an accident on the interstate. Being at a standstill on the interstate is no fun. Going 5-10 miles an hour, constantly stopping and starting, is no fun. This count it all joy situation is working patience on the inside. The trying of our faith works patience. Patience needs to have its perfect work in us that we may be entire wanting nothing (mature). Another incident involving patience may be standing in a long grocery line. Or, you may be experiencing another type of wait in your life. But, in each instance the wait is causing you to grow in ways you may not realize. As you are waiting on your answer from God, you will have more patience. It takes patience to wait on the promise! It's working for you. If you can think it's all going to work out in the end, you'll be alright. God saw the end from the beginning. We can't let our environment dominate us. We are in this world, but not of this world. We must check in with the Holy Spirit and let him speak to us in these times.

Some of you may be able to identify with this one, especially you baby boomers. Count it all joy when you can't remember your password and you're in a hurry. Now you've got to go through the process of verifying who you are. But, guess what? You've forgotten your security answers, too. This process has not only slowed you down, but now you're frustrated that you've lost so much time. Sometimes God will tell me "In your patience you possess your soul." We must have patience whether we want it or not. It's part of the fruit of the Spirit. I used to not want to pray for patience, because I knew what it entailed. I would get put in a real live test of my faith to produce more of it. It's part of the package. You've got to have it. So, if you've got to wait, have a pastime to work on. Sometimes, I find it's a good time to rehearse scripture. That way my mind is on God and He keeps me in perfect peace while I'm waiting.

Chapter 3
Jesus Did It

Jesus did it and He is our ultimate example to go by. He kept his focus. He was motivated to go through all the suffering and agony for us because he knew it would mean salvation for us. Beauty for ashes. For the joy that was set before Him, He endured the cross, despising the shame. Jesus kept his eyes on his future and that is what we should do.

You can do it, too! If God is for you who can be against you. (Romans 8:31) Despising the shame, keep your eyes on Jesus. Go through like Jesus. Keep your focus. He had a goal. His goal was to do the will of his Father. (John 6:38) Sometimes, you have to get rid of some deadweight, don't lean to your own understanding, and completely focus on what God is saying. He does have what you need. He has a plan for your life, plans to do you good and not evil. If you are willing and obedient, you will eat the good of the land. In other words, be willing to do what He says and when you do it, you will come out on top.

Speaking of being on top, are your goals pleasing to the will of the Father? You know the old saying, "What would Jesus do?" Are your intentions, thoughts, attitudes in line with what the Father wants for you?

Are you reaching the goals that you set? Or, do you get distracted and let the smallest thing that comes up throw you off? There are a lot of things out for your attention. Keep your focus. In all your ways acknowledge Him and He will direct your path. (Proverbs 3:6)

Everything it will take to get there - go through. Do it God's way! Just do it. There is joy at the end. Joy comes in the morning. (Psalm 30:5) The Word says, the sufferings of this present time are not worthy to be compared to the glory that shall be revealed in us whether in this life or eternally with our heavenly Father. (Romans 8:18) Joy is at the end, so just count it all joy.

In this hard situation of endurance, I about lost it! No joke! I ended up taking care of my husband and my mother at the same time, going from house to house. My husband had several ailments. High blood pressure, heart failure, and gout were the main ones. I was the one who had to tend to him like a nurse. God has a way of giving me my desires in ways I'm not thinking about it. I wanted to be a nurse when I was younger. Now I'm a nurse to my husband, my mother, and soon afterwards to a client. My mom had Alzheimer's and Parkinson's, a double whammy. This entailed a great deal. Someway, somehow God saw me through! You know God has a way of sending help when you need it most. I thank God for all the help he sent my way when my mom needed around the clock care. It was not easy. My husband had a heart attack and passed away. I found him on the floor after getting back home from taking my mom to the doctor.

The next day I moved in with my mom to give her my full attention since she needed it anyway. I guess I was in a state of shock, but I was thinking I could handle things as normal. I was even still making plans for our family reunion, but was talked out of it by my uncle. Sometimes we need wisdom to speak to us. My mom had episodes where she would have something like seizures and we would call the paramedics so many times. In fact, the same day my husband passed, she had three back to back sitting on the sofa. All I could say was, "Oh no!!!" I thought she was about to leave us, too. I thank God for my precious sister angel, LaCountess Kearney, who was there to pray for me. Sometimes I would even call her early in the morning to come pray for me. She helped me take excellent care of my mom. Not only her, but a few others to which I'm forever grateful. The reason I bring her up is that God had her there not only for my mother. But she was there for me, too. Sometimes when you're in a rough spot, you need some extra help. You need someone to lean on. God is always there, but He also works through others. He told me as we were discussing the Word one day, "Iron sharpens iron."

Soon after, I found myself in an ambulance rushing to the emergency room. I remember being admitted and a doctor walking into my hospital room. With my family around me, he bluntly said I could drop dead anytime. I was diagnosed with Hypertrophic Cardiomyopathy, which is also called Sudden Death Syndrome. But God!! This is not all of the story, it's only a little bit so you can see I had a lot going on. How can you say I should count this all joy? This was indeed a struggle! No doubt about it! But it brought about perseverance in me. Though he slay me yet will I trust Him. I had to put my mom in the nursing home for the last six months of her life because I couldn't even halfway make up my bed, let alone hers. But God is a deliverer! He delivered me! I was on medication, but was completely taken off and released. I'm not what I used to be. During this time the thing that I loved was hard to tolerate. When I was able to go back to church, I had to sit in the back because I couldn't handle the sound. I love the singing and the playing of the instruments. This was an adjustment now. Slowly, but surely, God turned things around.

God had a purpose in this situation for me to take care of the sick. I'm glad I had the opportunity to do so. With all its ups and downs and other oppositions, God saw me through. Looking back, I know God was preparing me for this season. I was working on a job as a programmer analyst and the contract ran out. I was thinking when one door closes another door opens. I was working on the mainframe computers, but now computers started going to personal computers and I needed some additional training. I found myself doing temporary work assignments. On one particular assignment, I was asked if I wanted to work the phones. I said, "No, I don't like the phones." I was asked to try it. I did, and ended up with a very nice office working for one of the head staff members at the

Virginia Housing Development Authority. This job was only 10 minutes from my mom's house and I was able to look in on her during lunch. Later on, they worked with me so I could have a flexible schedule. It was a blessing to be able to work half days there and still be able to take care of my mom the remainder of the day. As her illnesses progressed, I started taking care of her full time. God is so awesome. God has a way of doing things. He just does. Believe me, He has good plans for you. Even though it may not seem like good, it's working out for your good. I count it all joy because God was with me in it. Again, He saw the end from the beginning and ordered my steps. I developed other skills like managing and caring for people that I was able to carry over to another phase of my life that would sustain me. I have learned endurance through this and many other situations.

Since God is making it all work out for our good, we can say it's all good (Romans 8:28), and count it all joy. It's going to be ok. We will understand it better by and by. Look ahead in anticipation of what God has in store. Where He leads we follow. He knows the way and how to get there. I'm sure when the slaves were being led to freedom, it didn't feel so good going through the process, but in the end was very joyful, as they gained their freedom! Childbirth pains don't feel so good. But, after the birth! Birthing things out in the spirit is also labor, so push! Press toward the mark! In due season, you will reap if you faint not. What Jesus did for us was all worth it for us. He laid the foundation. All we have to do is follow the precepts. He wrote the book. We read the end. We just need to go through the process. Sometimes the things get hot, like the furnace of afflictions. (Isaiah 48:10) He is in the fire with you! Yea though I walk through the valley of the shadow of death I will fear no evil for thou art with me. (Psalm 23:4) God is with you! He will never leave you nor forsake you.

God is working in you what you need, to get you to where you need to be!

The next time you face a trial ask the Holy Spirit to help you through. Ask Him to show you strategies of what to do, what not to do, what to say, what not to say, and how to react. Ask Him to teach you

His ways. Know He is there to help you. Trust Him. God always gives a way of escape of every temptation after you have suffered a while. (I Corinthians 10:13) Be prayerful and stay in the Word. You will get through. Count it all joy! The joy of the Lord is your strength!

There is a song that goes like this, "This joy that I have the world didn't give it to me. This joy that I have the world didn't give it to me. The world didn't give it and the world can't take it away." So, go on through with a settled state of contentment. Go on through with confidence and hope. Go on through with cheerfulness. Go on through with gladness. Just draw from God's well of salvation. It will never run dry. No weapon formed against you will prosper. His strength is made perfect in your weakness. Count it all joy! Spread your wings and fly! Soar in the Spirit! He will perfect that which concerns you! (Psalm 138:8)

Our joy must be based on looking to God, the author and finisher of our faith. When you come out you can sing like me "I get joy when I think about what He's done for me!" Now take this joy that you have thinking about how He brought you through the last thing into the next thing. If He did it for you before, He can do it for you again.

Remember, God has a plan to prosper you and give you hope. You can count all things joy because God is with you and working on your behalf. You can count it all joy because He saw the end from the beginning. Nothing caught Him by surprise.

Concerning our situations, we don't always know how to pray as we ought, but Jesus Christ is at the right hand of the Father making intercession for us (Romans 8:34) and we also have the Holy Spirit making intercession for us (Romans 8:26), so all things...the good and the bad are working out for our good. God said, "Occupy until I come." We are more than conquerors through Jesus Christ! In the end "We Win," like my Chief Apostle Olive C. Brown always says. That's right, "We Win!" Fight the good fight of faith. God will see you through!

About the Author

Katrina B. Fonville resides in Richmond, Virginia. She studied at Virginia State University and J. Sargeant Reynolds Community College. She was married to the late Lynwood Earl Fonville, Sr., who passed away in 2005. She has three children, one stepchild, and four grandchildren.

She is part of the ministerial team at New Jerusalem International Christian Ministries where she serves faithfully. She enjoys outreach and helping those in need.

If you've enjoyed this book, please take a minute to give a brief rating and/or review on Amazon. The author can be reached via email at: katfonville@gmail.com.

Count It All Joy!

www.ingramcontent.com/pod-product-compliance
Lightning Source LLC
Chambersburg PA
CBHW060628030426
42337CB00018B/3254